DECLASSIFIED

MARIELA GRIFFOR

DECLASSIFIED

First published in 2017
by Eyewear Publishing Ltd
Suite 333, 19-21 Crawford Street
Marylebone, London W1H 1PJ
United Kingdom

Cover design and typeset by Edwin Smet
Author photograph by Elena Griffor
Printed in England by TJ International Ltd, Padstow, Cornwall

ISBN 978-1-911335-49-8

*Eyewear wishes to thank Jonathan Wonham for his
generous patronage of our press.*

WWW.EYEWEARPUBLISHING.COM

For Edward
whose presence demands
precision

TABLE OF CONTENTS

6

Give me a lever long
enough and a fulcrum on
which to place it, and I
shall move the world.
– Archimedes

I

Man is condemned to be free;
because once thrown into the world,
he is responsible for everything he does.

– Jean Paul Sartre

In the depth of the winter
I finally learned that there was in me
an invincible summer.

– Albert Camus

DECLASSIFIED

Entering I-75 towards Detroit for the first time was not easy.
Part of my deal was to stay no more than a year
with a visit to the National Archives.
I woke up with the vision of the hotel we would stay at.

Water was running from the ceiling
and, contaminated, was striking
the plastic head of the television.
In my dream I tried to wake them up.

When the children and my husband woke
I did tell them about the dream and they laughed.
No matter, I ran to the supermarket,
I bought gloves and disinfectant to clean up.

I put everything in the travel bag
in the trunk of our white Buick afterwards.
Now I was ready.
At the National Archives we needed to get badges.

I don't recall the section, the newly declassified materials
were stored in different rooms
so every time I needed to read a new period,
I filled in a new form. I don't know what I was looking for.

A name, a date, his name, somebody's name.
I was looking to save myself from that mirror.
Dispersed at large, we didn't belong to this world.
Five minutes before they closed, I found it.

At first, I felt like punching someone in the stomach,
like the punch the man in the September 4, 1985 protest gave me.
Exactly like that, give him back a few seconds
that seemed like hours without breathing,

then a very strange pulling like inside your brain,
like a flow of something, air or blood running out of you.
Then an incredible desire to throw up.
But they were there: across the table,

my two kids and my American husband;
they were drawing and he was reading more reports.
Their big innocent eyes knew something
had happened inside of me,

something that I could not talk about
but something important:
He knew the moment he saw my face;
he knew I had found what I was looking for.

The report continued with part of the name,
no code names, no aliases. They knew so little about him.
At least, there it was on the page, the name of *who they believe*
was responsible: Juan Manuel Contreras Sepulveda.

It was a surprise, I thought I would find more details.
I found a three page report that was supposed to help me
to find all the answers, a three page report with a third page
blacked out, a report that could have given me all the names,

including the name of who wrote it.
We went to the closest hotel. A 'Super 8' located in College Park.
We were planning to stay there one night.
At 3 a.m. a sound of dripping water woke me up

and I turned on the light and I could see
the water running through a fissure
that ran across the entire ceiling.
The children were sleeping in the second bed.

No one was amazed by my ridiculous look,
yellow gloves and two different products in my hands.
I started to clean, spraying everywhere.
Our oldest asked my husband, "How did Mom know?"

He responded, "No idea, she just knew!"
I asked them to go back to sleep and I assured them
we were out of danger and they needed to rest,
to which without complaint, they all obliged.

HISTORY OF A BED

First night? Or was it the second?

I still have the pillow case
and the sheets of the first
bed, rustic, little bit cheesy
with a big heart carved
in the headboard.

You had a double chin,
enough to be noticed.
Looking at you
sleeping from the door, when
I turned around, you were
glancing through an eye.

Who is this man?
Who is this man?
Maybe he is a prince who
would come to my rescue.
Who is this man?

Maybe he is not from here
but a Swede who wants to
be anonymous.
Who would like to be
there in a bed with a
wooden carved heart?
He doesn't want to
be anonymous.

The hair on the chest
was dark brown and heavy
I had never dated a man
with chest hair before.
Your nose, the prince nose, was
the most intriguing.

It took many months
for us to meet again.
Who is this man?
Who is this man?
There you were in a
bed that I gave to
my friend Violeta when I left.

If people only knew in Chile
that one member of one of their
best families inherited from
me a bed with a wooden
carved heart, they would laugh
until there is no tomorrow.
We will not tell them.

I know and have little wisdom now.
There is nothing that I don't know
from that body. We started
with the soul a long time ago.
I know it is so difficult to
talk about what happened but
we will try to take it slow.

MY HOUSE

My house is noisy, the TV is on,
the doorbell is ringing, the sound
of the arborvitae rubbing the
gutters is like spectral howling
in the middle of the day.

The dripping of that
drop of water has almost disappeared
but not quite yet, after two years.
He will fix that faucet someday.
There is always noise outside

the room, it is only here, where
I can see your photo, that
I don't find distractions. Your
photo, it's like my focal point.
Now the TV can be on and who

really cares if the arborvitae
tied to the post rubs the gutter
like a midday ghost.
I will jump into my past and find you,
find that time that still is here,

I will find that almost imperceptible smell
of bloodshot hearts that will evoke this
speechless city, the quiet sun,
the muted fog ascending over
my window, the strong odor

of the nearby Lake Saint Clair,
a minute away from the street,
the delirious denying from Grosse Pointe
contrasting with intermittent shots
coming from the streets of Detroit,

the nights the city brought us each day.
There is not so much more these
days, just a wish of no more
destruction and a desire to be
alone with this silence that can

be dangerous in its thinking.
There is always a possibility of
making the day better. I know deep
inside we've reached
a final point. I will be laughing, you will

not know how to fill the air
and I will be laughing. You
will turn on the TV, or the radio,
your specter dispersing
false statements of love and belonging

through this house. I will be sitting at my desk
trying to forget. There is no way back for us,
the minutes will be empty
and you will be desperate.
I will have no thoughts about time.

II

*The enchanting charms of this sublime science
reveal only to those who have the courage
to go deeply into it.*

— Carl Friedrich Gauss

*It is impossible to be a mathematician
without being a poet in soul.*

— Sofia Kovalevskaya

MATHEMATICAL POEMS

2 + 2 = REVOLUTION (NOT 4)

Put 4 people in a room:
more things
than 4 would happen.

UNIVERSAL CLOSURE

The universal closure
is not the end
but the beginning.

THE FORGETFUL FUNCTOR

The forgetful functor
must ultimately remember
where it comes from
before all the details
are thrown away!

ALGEBRA OF INTERACTION

The algebra of
Interaction
is unity,
one,
or identity.

IN ADDITION

In addition,
our unity is zero.

BETWEEN POETS

There is no identity
operation
between poets.
There is no poet
whose interaction
with another poet
would leave either poet
the same,
not even if
the poet is dead.

POETS AND APPLES

One poet + one apple
is still just one poet,
does this mean
that apples are the identity
for poetic interaction?

THE IDENTITY POET

What is the identity for
poetic interaction?
Whatever else
it is not a poet.
Whatever it is that
doesn't change interaction.

POEM

I love you.
You are my 1/3.
You will
never be my better half.

III

There is no remedy for love but to love more.

– Henry David Thoreau

Love loves to love love.

– James Joyce

We should meet in another life,
we should meet in air, me and you.

– Sylvia Plath

IN SEARCH OF MOTHS

For F. W.

How was F looking for some comfort
in the heart of his wife without noticing that she didn't
even care about his search? It was kind of cruel
to have met in the high school and for years to call
each other sweetheart because the sweetheart
was not living there anymore. Her mind moved out
years ago when money was no longer enough and
the payment due at the end of the month broke her heart;
she didn't know about real needs until she met him.
Her body stayed with them. There were too many needs.
This cruelty would not be pardoned by her own family
and friends and she did care what they thought about her.

★★★

F was asking himself:
When and where do you find less or more truth
in what your friends are telling you:
at the beach or at the sharper edge of a kitchen table
or on a yellow tablecloth on an old beach,
or inside naked bodies in a bed full of the untold
or a cold winter night at the exit of a bar,
at the end of the blue street of a city full of blood?
When do you find this common experience,
of a sacrilege or an offense or a simple human error
that converts you into a closer ally of obscurity,
stretched out on one of those homeless couches
more truthful than the rain you touch or the poison you drink?

★★★

"What then?" I asked him if I should pray,
and he laughed with a turbulent sound
that shook all the true bugs hanging on the wall:
the Japanese giant hornet, the Hemipteran,
the wasp, the locusts, the siafu, the fire ants,
the fleas, the Anopheles mosquito, the moths:
Above all this clarity, the seed of a new life
faraway from the black forest turned into light:
Nothing existed without that pestilent past,
but a drop of dignity fighting inside,
wanting to fly from the crushed lineage:
"No, you should not pray." Greater glory in my pests.

★★★

It was not a white angel
or bird or even
inner map that kept
F going, but a tangle
of voices, tiny voices,
coming and coming
like a scream from a quiet
euphoria. He found himself
standing at the door,
in a hollow day, cicadas
reminding him of who he was.

★★★

She crept through the corridors
between the two buildings close
to the Berlin Public Library: Happy
to go back and buy fresh raisin bread

in the morning. Overseas nobody cared about
the fresh bread, but here it was a "must"
to eat bread in the morning. F was not with her,
so the flame of who she had been was encrusted in
the wine cup: Metallic, cool, impersonal but unnerving:
No tears shed in the second month either.

***

And so the voices appeared:
"All right," he mumbled
and found nothing but himself.
The last thing he remembered
was that she squeezed the back
of his neck. Just like old times.
She will be busy with an almost
empty bottle and her drawings.
When she steps into them, she will
not think about him at all. F
knew more than this: Oblivion will
roll its ocean and the home syllable will drown.

***

His insects will not matter
at least for one day: After all
they were hanging on the wall: Dead.
Should a man and his soul step into an
empty room or should a dazzling stone
from the past visit the world? All of this
was clear to him once but not today.
Today was different. His iron shoes
were not moving. His face
was glued to the gates of her silence.

The end was near and a soul-eclipsed-moon
marked the beat counting.

***

Tell me when it hurts,
or if you are ready, he wanted to ask her.
(You live as if you will live forever but you won't).
He wondered if that would start to move
her, push her away, slowly like
the spume coming from the sea.
They sealed
their friendship and made a pact:
We need to find a fine tuning to
this new life: "Does it hurt?"
"Are you ready?"
She said, "Never." Painfully.

***

It did not flash out. She was always
grateful for all he did for her. He was torn
apart when she told him. The empty bed
will not be empty. He would not
have to hunt anymore. He resented her
for just a second. It will be summer again,
and it will be raining soon but he was
not thinking about that right now:
He knows he will never let go.
Love can have strange twists:
Their destiny should be kept secret.

***

27

The rain, stepping in day after day after day.
They slept in the same room each night,
remembering the time when they were teenagers.
They blamed their parents for keeping them
separated sometimes, but at the end they laughed.
Nobody could keep them apart for a long time.
They were burning leaves otherwise: What was
happening to her? The flowers in the garden appear to go on
forever and the night seems to be a contagious ward
afflicted with a hopeless longing that never arrives.

★★★

He dreams and he is angry. This beginning
is uglier, more true. It is natural to be tired, walking
around like a lost insomniac, lost in that place
that they built together. This new self
is more metaphysical. She regrets having left him for
those months when she ran to Vienna.
What was she expecting to happen there?
He is angry for those months she stole from him.
Now things were different, more balanced.
They were not performers, now they knew
the darkness hurt, harmed.

★★★

Yes. She wanted to be touched,
with tenderness and with the memories of
who she was. It would make her feel good.
The past floated over her skin
and she felt like the edges of a river but more lifelike,
like crowding the water with its own substance.
There were no worries there but the leaves

were issuing a subtle request for pity.
Her disappearance was noticed by the air
so the weather and the ground grew bitter, just enough.

★★★

They were born, they were more than one:
From the petrified face they have their roots
born here in this paralyzing premise of union

that was no union but desire from their drifting
bodies something like a dust cloth over the world,
over their quest for answers.

They were real, like
a great train terminal full of people but
lonely. She kept only one dream: To hear his mouth shut

and she wanted to be herself ten years ago when she was
complete and still young. They wanted each other
so much with that hunger from yesterday, from

that solitude and mistrust that navigated inside of them
with no purpose but the irony of complaint: After all
his best poem was not her or his bugs but his "little something."

★★★

He was always sick: Sometimes so were the bugs
hanging on the walls. Sometimes, his father who
kept him away. His mind changed with the moon,
with an empty glass, with banshees or the eyesight
of a cat disregarding him, as if the world
was ending without rewarding him.

What could have been otherwise?

He could have been a scholar, a baker, a drunk,
a serious drunk, a soldier, it would not have mattered
if not for that intellect going down there in the abyss
of a home inhabited by too many bugs, cats,
too much bathyspheric coldness;
he needed to sing, he needed to survive, arise.

★★★

And now and then he called me to yell
over the phone.
I never knew who he was when he did that.
Phantoms, phantoms,
always phantoms, like whirling flames,
over my ears, my mouth,
my soul. And then silence:

A foaming dark layer of silence covering me
from head to toe. Can you imagine?
Calling to this little something!
That call is growing now inside of me like a mixture
of saffron and acid, like a bright wing of an archetype,

like the head of a three dimensional thought
that will shape him into a hysterical
scene. I sit there in my kitchen without judging him.
I hang up the phone. Pull it out.
I distract my mind one more time.

★★★

She too was crazy at times
but her courage was equal to her craziness:

Who else could have lived with him
for so long: Loving him, hating him,

laughing, oh my dear here, oh my hero there,
barren words at times, for the most part he had become a burden.

Not to me though (this little something can carry it all).
We can be reckless and soft, all at once, and sing rhyme

after rhyme, sing beat upon beat in an accelerated
time that can destroy any form or transform any mind.

★★★

Despite stern waves of time she thought she loved him.
Who could not love this poor little thing
that could not do better than to link forgotten syntax.
This thing that could be a glorious piece of heaven

when he was clear. He was a poisonous ballad of
blood craving mouths that could destroy any army
at other times. He could enter under the skin of anybody but me.
She hated it, she knew this little something would be accumulating

his broken pieces, his swamps of lightness and would dissect him
in a gaudy verse, an ancient tomb, a fiesta of pagan words
and make him live in a succeeding
ripple of thoughts and she was afraid.

31

★★★

I kept most of what I thought about him
for myself. He went in and she went out.
Both were trapped in my danger,

I glued them to my web like his creepy crawlies.
That slim civilization reclining in her soul
was slouching towards an absurd natural conclusion.

What could she have found
at 4 a.m. when she ran to the church?
What was she praying for? A big loud beast was running
out of convictions, with a passionate doubt.

She wanted to make sense of all her sacrifices, pardon him,
remain in God, yet flying into this new and uncommon
lowliness. She was entering the psalms in her own
final justice: Unnoticed as a cat.

IV

I think to be in exile is a curse, and you need to turn it into a blessing. You've been thrown into exile to die, really, to silence you so that your voice cannot come home. And so my whole life has been dedicated to saying, "I will not be silenced".

– Ariel Dorfman

No exile at the South Pole
or on the summit of Mont Blanc separates us
more effectively from others than the
practice of a hidden vice.

– Marcel Proust

THE VOICE

Where is your house? she asked.
My house is in the
refugee camp, I told her.

Where are your parents? she asked.
In a country far away,
my mother is still alive but
my father died for everyone's silence.

What language do you speak?
All of them, I replied.
My language is wet
sand in the fingers,
the bricks of my house:
it is looking for an army.

RECOVERY

May 20, 2014

For Regina Derieva

We never met; we never spoke to each other
except through the immigrant song of Jan Johansson,
we knew we were united in
indestructible fibers of life breathing
in and breathing out, marching
to the sound of old days, in countries
that remind us of our own countries,
speaking old languages, that remind us of our own tongues,
we became so suddenly eternal tourists with a right to vote.

It was a time in my life when I stopped laughing
and I knew you did too. I could see it
in the photographs of magazines and
journals where new poems by you were published.
I knew what it was to be without a reason to laugh.

So very sorry to have to miss you,
well-planned journeys, well they never happened.
I planned several trips to Rinkeby,
a town that I avoided fiercely when
I was there. It is not easy
to be reminded of cut wings, as you know.

My trips to Stockholm were always
the same, *Gamla Stan*, centrum, H&M
and the Viking Museum, then back to Uppsala.
Rinkeby was a forbidden point,
the limbo of anybody's trajectory.
But had I known then you were there

I would have faced the fear
and visited you.

I love your work. The fresh, naïve
and sweet idea the world can be improved, stained
on the pages everywhere.
I love the way you put the
best of you in your poems. The way
you make yourself at home inside a whale,
the way some of your images cannot
leave my head for days, exactly like
a pop song. The way you make me think
with each line and take me to places
I have never been before.

I love the way that insufferable persistence
of something must change in this
endlessness of war times, this time that
consumes each of us and makes us bend
in the direction of the wind a dozen times per day
as in your poem. I pray for that persistence
to infect everyone who reads you.

I'm sorry to have missed you in this life.
I imagine what great times you and I would have had
if we only had the opportunity and time, and money of course,
don't forget that, to meet.

Silly of me to think we would have had
that cup of coffee in *Gamla Stan*
and talked about pigeons and old catholic schools,
and how the world is not changing but ending.
Nature has its tricks, and even if we make progress,
it will make us part of its garden. Yes, at least.

BEFORE AND AFTER

The first time she died, She killed herself in Her heart
        the second time was pure hell taking its course.

They couldn't find the love in common
        nor was She devotional nor easy to handle.

She was a luminous storm, tongue and thorns
                and She inherited a certain rough quality.

                She preferred small doses of her sparks.
Could it be possible they were all mistaken?

Is this the same for everybody?
or had She been misled by her post-partum gale?

For sure She will find a little bit of sweet honey
                mixed in with an ocean of cruelty.

They weren't meant for each other.
                Was She born too soon or too late?

In many ways this search has only one way it can go
                and She arrives always at the same point.

She is not there where She put herself.
        She glides like a jelly-fish following her own course.

Now when She has already expired
                She has a chance to find herself.

She wishes for a tear to close this cycle,
                something warm and meaningful

to clean up the mascara off her messy cheeks.
　　　　Could it be possible She had become this shattered?

She knew the light was there, clattering with hygienic care,
　　　　the tragedy of her mother's empty shoes.

BIRTHDAY POEM FOR MY MOTHER

I would like to settle
a friendship with you.
Open doors made of veils,
an age without weight
and forget the heavy absence
of those years.
In my exile I've forgotten
my natural tongue,

I haven't forgotten the sound
of your steps,
even less the sound of our ocean.
I learned at your school
everything has an order:
antibiotics for a virus,
alcohol for bacteria.
I am far away now,

my reason for tears
is the first and the last,
my disease, my diphtheria.
How do you erase the memory
from those who only remember?
What is it like
to dive into a troubled sea?
You silence me and I have to start over.

In proud fury you say
I regret nothing,
for appearance and duty
I look for you but find nothing

in this remote basement,
this lonely cellar.
How can an empty body walk,
without choices,

with a Medusa's pain
touching others with hard mischief?
Don't judge me, he already has.
I begged, pleaded but he wanted nothing.
Could it be the other son
that scraped at your bowels,
made your heart a frozen puddle,
that coral smile and hummingbird body.

God took away his life
and he took it away from you.
Is this the reason you're cold within?
The beaten egg marks your injured door.
I listen to the wind sigh a little
then whistle slowly.
It tells me the little bird is at peace,
reclining on the sweet

skirt of your lap, asleep forever
in the maternal gentleness
that shapes your arms.
Dust your sadness into the air.
Let the whole world cover itself
in our misery.
Mother, mother, I call for you
and as always, you are never there.

(Translated from Spanish by Karla Cordero and Jesus Esparza)

THE LAST ONE

Last night I could not sleep,
the children were not at home. They both had
sleepovers. I was tired, too. Too much time away from
grown ups and I know they will be OK, I will move
back. This time, closer to my father, that at that
time will be old and probably very cranky. But
I will move back to spend with him the
time we never could give to each other before.
I will move back to those mountains in between
Pucon and Talcahuano, I will go to the beaches
around. I also plan to write.

I will take walks in San Pedro to
meet those people I saw the last time
when I was there, and I will run to the
Ocean, to touch the black sand of San Pedro,
I will be closer to God, feeling the thick
air of the early morning. I will let the salt
make my face ruggy and I will think about you and
those days in Chiloé, at the End of the Earth.
I also will go and visit my old relatives, those
that are so old that they don't even remember their
ages. I will put back the pieces of that last poem, and
will promise that you will always have a place in my mind.

It's time for you and me to go different
ways. You find the place your soul was longing.
And I will choose to stay here without you and
with the other I love. Just hang out there,
the day to get together is every day shorter,
but now it is time for me to do so much more.

Last night as I said I could not sleep
I knew this would be my last letter and my
last poem for you.

V

If you talk to a man in a language he understands, that goes to his head. If you talk to him in his language, that goes to his heart.

– Nelson Mandela

Language is a virus from outer space.

– William S. Burroughs

But if thought corrupts language, language can also corrupt thought.

– George Orwell

TRANSITIONING LANGUAGES

The evening of August 23th, 1999 was foggy
and very dark. You did not expect a better
winter that year. Michigan was
the last place on the planet where you wanted
to be. It was very clear to me
after a year and half that we
would stay there for a long time.

The professor turned off
the television and now he was talking
about Revolution. The mass media
survey class had around sixty
students. He asked a couple of
questions and nobody answered. He picked
a name. Who was the dictator
of Chile from 1973 to 1989? He asked.
Silence: The person signaled they did not know.
Augusto Pinochet, you said timidly,
Very good, he said and
he talked about the video and how
the media act in political conflicts.

Your body was shaking and your hands
moving, trembling.
It was stupid! Stupid, you said to
Me: To talk when
I don't even understand
what he is saying.
You felt your heart ready to
explode and you left for the bathroom.
There, you cried and let the emotions

come out. You washed your face.
You drank water and walked back
to the room.

It was difficult to be
in Lessenberry's class. He was
a monster: He could make
anybody talk and not *off the record*.
Fortunately you never did find out about
his dark side. After the class Katty and you waited
for him. Katty had a crush on him
from the first moment and she
asked you to stay.
There the interview began:
And who are you? he asked.
You told him a devastating but short
story about yourself,
and a new life in another language started.

FIRST ENCOUNTER

She laughed at the complications
and the extensions of an unexpected
grammar. She spelled:

> Te Amo!
> I love you!
> Je t'aime!

in case he knew any of these languages.

CHAMBERS

'And thou thyself, Calliope.'
– Sappho

For Urban Lundberg

I

Place of amber and gold
where he as a shark rises:
Let no bounds keep us in
garments of greed and no fun!
Let these men's thoughts sway free.

II

I have measured my defeat
a hundred times, at the edge
of his grave but clearly,
under your potent flames,
the wall does not crumble.

III

Behold the red bells
for you will need them,
keep your *blå-sippor*, they
will crash further
in your leaderless hand.

IV

The "Lady of the Books" –
he baptized her, working
on the prison of his fields,
stealing infamous mortality
from the Sundial's Bofors.

V

Bright yellow and blue
star incomparable beyond
limits exposed like scars.
How many glorious predestined sites
fall each day under your glow?
"We have taken lives and saved many more."

VI

Are you really alive
under your dirty skin?
Who commands your battles?
Who kills in your name?
At what time of the day do you
perfect your machines?

VII

You, treacherous, secret little wisdom
learned at the very Royal Institute of Technology,
computed profits of low essence
citadel of swelling fragments
Kakelugn of scattered fathers and sons.

VIII

Somewhere on the borders
of *Lilliput* and *Blefuscu*
your mouth is salivating
with their lives.

IX

I will wait until
the mountains can talk
until the ground tells
me where his voice crumbled.
I will drink from his last breath,
O, you inspire, you inspire me
to know your name.

X

I will connect all the pieces
of his memory in your Cathedrals.
I will speak only with his voice
so you feel the terror, hunted,
populated by mother earth's trembling anger.
I will know all your names and sing them
in a hymn of immortal cries.

XI

I stand in a dark alley
trying to pour out light
from this hollow carcass.
I litter a wreath of disaster
leaking shadows wherever I go.
All that remains is the time the sun swallowed.

XII

I know this Great River should be prudent:
as all the great rivers it wants to run free
unconditional and with faithful followers:
The Shark will not swallow all the waters or men.
I will wait for you, sharpening an action between
my index finger and my thumb.

VI

They laugh at me because I'm different; I laugh at them because they're all the same.

– Kurt Cobain

Everything I ever let go of has claw marks on it.

– David Foster Wallace

BEFORE

Miguel and his sisters were regular assistants in the Catholic Church in San Pedro. He had invited her many times to his church but she refused until one day he invited her to one of those bibles studies, those bible studies! Miguel was waiting for her at the entrance of the church. She and Miguel crossed the long building and went behind the church to a tiny office beside the parish house.

Five other youths were inside and two of them were in the process of putting a thick, black blanket on the window to block out the light. The room was completely dark and one of them turned the light on. A man with a beard and glasses came into the room with a video that he left on the table where he sat, waiting for the group to take their seats.

Miguel sat beside her and told her not to worry, nothing bad would happen. She was the only girl in the group. The man with the beard opened the box with the video and played it on the small black and white TV located at the other end of the table.

The man started and said: "Dear Comrades ... In the name of the Leftist Revolutionary Movement, I thank you today for your attendance to this important meeting ..." and then he said: "What you will watch today are scenes from our country and what happens to our people..."

She was sweating and her knees were shaking. Miguel sat beside her and asked if she wanted a drink of water. She told him that she needed one. He disappeared and was back moments later with a glass of water from inside the church. The man was still talking and moving as he talked. He asked that they turn off the lights as he started the video. The pictures of the Government House destroyed and pictures of bodies in the basement lined up by the dozens.

Nobody spoke or said anything. She felt a dry cough coming in her throat and the cold water calmed the itching. When the video was over she wanted to get outside immediately but Miguel asked her to wait until the bearded man left. She waited there, meanwhile the man picked up his video and shook hands with the others in the group.

He came directly to her and asked her how old she was? *Fifteen*, she told him, *thank you* he said, and shook her hand. He left in seconds. The others in the group disappeared as soon as the man left. Miguel told her to wait until he returned the TV to one of the priests in the church. She had the sensation of being in a different world. She imagined that the meeting was a sort of dream and it never happened.

Outside, the weather was hot and dry. They walked to her house but she did not let Miguel come in. She told him she was tired and she wanted to rest. They could have gone out later with the others and had an ice cream, in truth she wanted to get rid of him.

The next couple of days she avoided him. Miguel seemed to be hiding something from her. The basement images came to mind many times. The books and the speech of the president that her grandfather let her hear on the radio. She never saw images of the basement of the Stadium though. Miguel was like somebody different now. He also had something to hide like everybody else around her.

How was it possible to live in a place where everybody was hiding something, when the fact of hiding something was the only difference between those who she knew well and those whom she didn't?

Maybe the others whom she didn't know as well as the boys in the meeting also hid something or were going to do something like Miguel. After Miguel talked her into returning to the bible studies, she realized it was still a mistake. What did she know about bodies in a basement? She was then the president of her high school because Rosa Gonzalez, her English teacher, had nominated her.

They all went to a party where they saw the videos from the Stadium basement. She did cry this time. There nothing was unknown. They got drunk, with blank childhood faces they suddenly adopted. They blew up the entire city in only three months.

DERIVATIVES
for Elena

I told her to take Ruca to the backyard
to play with his new toys, the plastic
stick smelling of bacon
and the squeaky red ball.

She opened the kitchen door,
took the bonelike stick
and cast it into the air, with all her
might – the stick first, then the ball.

Then, the dog ran out.
I saw them playing like when she was little,
running back and forth without the pressure
of a future and only good memories

of a near past.
Ruca behaves in many ways like Matilda
– buried at the foot of the pine –
happy and gentle, oblivious to

the rabbits and squirrels running away from him,
afraid of a stampede of soft
laughter and insignificant barks.
Through the window I made him

aware of the duck couple flying over
the water and staying there for three days
as they have been doing for these
last twenty-two years.

I told her to be careful
but they could not hear me.
For years I hated this house,
all the struggle to repair the roof,

the kitchen, the bathrooms
and the enormous pool from the Fifties
we inherited from the old owners.
I put so much effort into this house

that I cannot remember all of it.
For twenty-two years I tried
to figure out how to
stay one more year. It was

always too big for a family
of four and gigantic, almost, for
just two of us.
She picked up the bacon stick

went to the end of the yard and as
in the past she ran with the dog
to the corner of the pool where
the duck couple emerged from

the water, lifting their wings over
the air into our neighbor's
fence and then yard.
Ruca barking over the fence,

her splashing tiny little stones over
the surface of the swimming pool
as she used to do over the ocean somewhere.
I didn't know where her mind was,

over what Atlantic corner reliving
memories important only to her.
She walked to the fence, grabbed the toys
and called the dog while she moved

closer to the house.
How long had passed, five minutes?
Good boy! she told him and bent over
to pet him on the head.

Anybody can have this house, anybody
can put a price on it, buy it or sell it.
It is not the house that yields truth and love.
The purpose of staying was this moment.

HARDSHIP

Somebody told me this country was hard:
But not this hard.
I didn't believe it because
I came from a hard country myself
and because I lived in other hard
countries so I was not afraid.
I thought we were different yet not
that different. I have nostalgia
for the homeland as I always
did have nostalgia so it was
nothing new. When I started
to see and feel in this new
spooky way and my left eye
started to tremble and I could not
control the movement, like the
most embarrassing tic you can
imagine, I withdrew. The time
began to walk slowly in the
inside and very fast on the outside.
The day after the new election
the bombs and the new troops
didn't stop, we will not talk
about it, because as in my hard
country we don't talk about it.
We can talk only about what
we can talk about and the
rest is just the poor imagination
of dissidents. And how can it be
interesting to talk about what
dissidents talk about if
we already talked about it in the past

election in the last century. It was
always the same. I do try to see the
good side of living in a hard country
though, so I'm not totally a critic.
I do want to have
my duties, my opinions, and I do
want to see things are changing for
the better, including the economy as
they say on TV. One of the good things
when soldiers come from the front line.
Have you seen the screen of the TV full
of beautiful children running to meet
daddy or mommy coming back? And
the uniform they wear, really beautiful,
no marks of blood or dirt anywhere.
Nobody could guess what
those uniforms can say. Don't take
this the wrong way. I also come
from a family in another hard
country that knows very well
the duty and honour of wearing a uniform
especially this one. What hits me
the hardest is the bouquet
of flowers the soldier brings to his
bride or wife and the running of
this beautiful woman to his side,
the crying every time. Perhaps because
I'm a romantic and I like flowers
or perhaps because I remember his
face destroyed by the hand grenade
he was carrying or the landmine
put in the ground by who knows who.
I guess we will never know. I remember
thinking how much makeup

the mortician had to put
over his face to hide all that
damage. His hair looked good
but those nostril pieces missing
will haunt me forever. See? My
country is also hard. Like
yours. I do think there is
a reason sometimes, yet
most of the time I just think
there is a bigger plot and not
exactly by God or the Devil that things
are this hard. Those who don't
think I'm right, they tell me
to get over it, to adapt, to adjust
and get over it. The ones that think
I'm right, they are mostly silent,
they hide, they don't like my
posts and they avoid
me when I get too difficult.
The problem is that I cannot
adapt and I'm always surprised
seeing more and more people
give in. Yesterday my oldest
child told me in the grocery store
she hated Albanians. *Why?* I asked
her and she told me, in her building
on the first floor there is a family
of four living in a nine hundred square foot
apartment and all above them can
smell their disgusting food,
bending over to my ear she whispered
and said, *I don't like them because they
are all terrorists. And how do you know
that?* I asked. *Everybody knows that*

she responded looking over her
shoulder to show me the Albanian couple
paying at the next cashier. I tell
her that's it. No more. I know I
will adapt. I will write more things
that can be printed and some people
will never read my poems and maybe
I will not think this country is hard
anymore and I will see the positive
side of the whole story and forget.
In the meantime I don't, I'm dangerous
if I remember scars, doorbells,
the sulfur smell of the tear gas
bomb and whistling zig-zag of
bullets coming from an unknown
direction, or if I remember he didn't
have his three left hand fingers.
[But excuse me for a moment,
my friend Cora is at the door,
we need to chat about her French doors
she is getting for her house]
Back to what I was saying:
He used to play the guitar with that hand.
I know they told me this
country was hard but I'm telling
you the truth when I say, nobody
really told me it was this hard.

PREPARATION

April 20, 2014

He is sitting in the garden with
a cigarette in his mouth,
a cup of coffee in the other hand.
With his left hand he plays
the tip of the cigarette over his lips,
rolling it over his mouth.
The cell phone on speaker is
on the table and a voice that
is barely recognizable comes from
the phone via invisible waves.
I sit inside the house in my study
and try to write some pieces of
my day. Where to start? Nina
baked an entire Holy Week
meal for sixteen of us. She made
the bread exactly like her grand-
mother used to bake in Bavaria.
He brought his friend from work
so not to leave him alone this day.
Our children were with other
friends and relatives, they decided
not to come in a clear sign of
emancipation. The voice from the
phone speaker is Ernie's. He is
alone again. His wife left for
Germany for four or five months,
he promised to follow but we all
know he will not go until the end
of that long vacation or retirement.
I will sit and enjoy the meal

as in the past when grandmother
was making the meal. This time I will not
recognize the language or really I
could not remember if it was Palm Sunday
or Good Friday the days I had
the most fun when I was little.
Sometimes it was not that fun,
it was not fun
because we were not allowed to listen
to TV or radio, run or play or
distract the meditative states that
grandmother and grandfather went
into suddenly. I don't know what
was worse, the time nearing
Palm Sunday or before. I know
Palm Sunday was OK because I
enjoyed the procession, the people in
church and the laughter of
children. I well remember Palm
Sundays. The day before we could
have the bouquet blessed. There was
no other day so special for me
as the day before Palm Sunday.
We sat at the table and we braided
braids and we put the bouquets
on top of each other. I knew they
would be blessed by the priest with
holy water and the water would splash
onto my clothes and I would feel that
special, splashed by the water blessed
by the Holy Spirit. Amazing how
things can change over the years.
When J. died I prayed all day, I
prayed and I bit the nose of Saint

Mary because it was so close to
my mouth and without controlling
my nerves I bit her nose first and
the side of her face, tearing apart
her left ear. The plastic was not so
hard. When I finally discovered
I had bitten her face I felt bad, guilty of
such stupidity, more annoyed by
my own neglect than anything else.
Often I did things that I was not
completely aware of, like this one
or like wearing and walking
in shoes on the wrong side
until my feet hurt. People
laugh at my distractions but
I would not be able to share this
indiscretion, like biting the nose and
ear of the Holy Mary plastic figure.
No, they would think I was crazy.

FLOW

April 22, 2014

Sometimes I want to hurry
to write you some poems before you die
so you can read them and we can
talk and laugh at the moment.

I want to find the tender side
of the stone wall in all our fights.
So we fill those hollow places with
some healing words.

I love you, as simply and deeply
as I can. In all these languages
that separate me from you, I do
have to tell you this so you understand.

I live life rapidly and you take your time.
How many lives can we draw together
at this pace? It is our secret how
I 'wind' down to fit the waltz.

No amount of seasons could explain
how this river of love flourishes
and beats with two hearts or how we
survive the clashes of our minds each year.

We live with the Seine behind or the crazy
sizzling of the Maipo River,
we leave behind old weight and ghost birds
to meet in this dimension where layers

of words and silences bring us a moon
or a sun on a good day.

THANK YOU NOTE

I'm grateful for my two daughters, you my husband,
my grandchild, my son-in-law, my new little dog, my
senses and my health, my books, my poems, my poems.
my poems, my languages, my language, my thoughts,
my love, the Universe, my literary hand, the power to
bless and be blessed, my books in Spanish, my books
in English, my books in any language that I can read
and cannot read yet, the power to understand, thanks
for healing, healing, healing, healing, love, the day, the
night, my house, my neighbors, my friends, my critics,
my family, my food, her food, the food of others, my
opportunities, the courage, my forgiveness, my illusions,
my dreams, my goals, my world, I'm grateful for the
plants, the birds, the air, the sun, this paper, this paper,
this pen, this pen, this love, this love, I'm grateful for my
cup of tea, the bright oranges, the sweet honey, the day,
always grateful for the day, always the light, the words,
always the words, for you, for him, for her, for them,
for all of us, the past, the present, the future, this sun,
this teaching, the opening of my heart, the opening of
their hearts, the opening of their minds, our minds, my
art, my voice, myself, my simple me, my complex me,
their complex selves, their simple selves. I'm grateful
for this moment, all the moments, for more words, for
more poems, for more love, for the forest, the sea, the
memories, the sky, always the sky. For you, who brought
me here.

ACKNOWLEDGEMENTS

The author would like to thank the following publications where these poems have appeared: *Passages North, Antonin Artaud Publications, Poetry International, Texas Poetry Review, Curator Aquarum Anthology* and *Poetry Anthology Tupelo Press 2015*. Thanks to Todd Swift and Edwin Smet for bringing this book into the world.

**EYEWEAR** PUBLISHING

EYEWEAR'S TITLES INCLUDE

EYEWEAR
POETRY

KATE NOAKES CAPE TOWN
SIMON JARVIS EIGHTEEN POEMS
ELSPETH SMITH DANGEROUS CAKES
CALEB KLACES BOTTLED AIR
GEORGE ELLIOTT CLARKE ILLICIT SONNETS
HANS VAN DE WAARSENBURG THE PAST IS NEVER DEAD
BARBARA MARSH TO THE BONEYARD
DON SHARE UNION
SHEILA HILLIER HOTEL MOONMILK
MARION MCCREADY TREE LANGUAGE
SJ FOWLER THE ROTTWEILER'S GUIDE TO THE DOG OWNER
AGNIESZKA STUDZINSKA WHAT THINGS ARE
JEMMA BORG THE ILLUMINATED WORLD
KEIRAN GODDARD FOR THE CHORUS
COLETTE SENSIER SKINLESS
ANDREW SHIELDS THOMAS HARDY LISTENS TO LOUIS ARMSTRONG
JAN OWEN THE OFFHAND ANGEL
A.K. BLAKEMORE HUMBERT SUMMER
SEAN SINGER HONEY & SMOKE
HESTER KNIBBE HUNGERPOTS
MEL PRYOR SMALL NUCLEAR FAMILY
ELSPETH SMITH KEEPING BUSY
TONY CHAN FOUR POINTS FOURTEEN LINES
MARIA APICHELLA PSALMODY
TERESE SVOBODA PROFESSOR HARRIMAN'S STEAM AIR-SHIP
ALICE ANDERSON THE WATERMARK
BEN PARKER THE AMAZING LOST MAN
MANDY KAHN MATH, HEAVEN, TIME
ISABEL ROGERS DON'T ASK
REBECCA GAYLE HOWELL AMERICAN PURGATORY
MARION MCCREADY MADAME ECOSSE
MARIELA GRIFFOR DECLASSIFIED
MARK YAKICH THE DANGEROUS BOOK OF POETRY FOR PLANES
HASSAN MELEHY A MODEST APOCALYPSE

EYEWEAR
LITERARY
CRITICISM

MARK FORD THIS DIALOGUE OF ONE - WINNER OF THE 2015 PEGASUS
AWARD FOR POETRY CRITICISM FROM THE POETRY FOUNDATION
(CHICAGO, USA).